WHAT EVERY FAMILY MUST KNOW

ULTIMATE WORKBOOK FOR SMOOTH SUCCESSION AND ESTATE PLANNING

CA PAWAN KR AGARWAL

INDIA • SINGAPORE • MALAYSIA

ISBN
Hardcase 979-8-89673-328-7
Paperback 979-8-89632-754-7

CONTENTS

INTRODUCTION

Continuous Improvement Is

Better Than Perfect Inaction

INTRODUCTION

You have worked hard throughout your life. You have a number of assets like stocks, real estate, metals, legal rights etc. These assets are immortal but a man is mortal. So you must maintain your records meticulously to ensure smooth succession. Succession planning is ignored by most of us, thus putting the legal heirs in insurmountable difficulties in getting inventory of all your assets. Not only assets, your heirs must know what your liabilities are and a host of other information. This chapter will help you in organizing your state of affairs in a systematic way to ensure effortless succession after you pass on.

If you are in a business or profession you have to have a plan for continuing of the same by way of proper succession planning. Often disputes occur after the death of a person among his heirs as to the entitlement of his estate. Proper documents will help in avoiding conflicts and litigation.

It is equally important that your successor preserves your values, belief, culture and tradition. For example, you have set up a charitable trust which is rendering yeoman service to the society. Would you not like to continue the same beyond your life from generation to generation? Often such organisation faces problems after the demise of the settlor or trustees.

The whole idea is to keep the entire information handy so that your successor does not run helter skelter when you are no more there to assist.

How to use this work book

To get most out of this work-book, follow the below mentioned guidelines:-

1. Don't use gel pen as ink from it takes longer time to dry on the paper. They also tend to skip across the surface even with very light pressure. Instead use a normal ball pen.
2. Before writing in the workbook, note down in a rough notebook. Review it and once you are sure that the information is correct, write the same in this workbook.
3. If you have no information about certain points, keep it blank at this moment. You may fill it up afterward as and when you gather the required details.
4. Review your work-book every year and make the necessary changes.
5. Keep the work book in lock and key but ensure that the same is available to those for whom it is meant.
6. Also maintain a parallel file where you can keep further details which are voluminous. For example, your demat account details, your holdings, name and address of depository participants (DP) or mutual funds may be mentioned in this work book, but detailed list of all your investments can be kept in a separate file. Similarly, details of insurance policies may be recorded in the notebook, but the insurance policies may be kept in a separate master file.
7. You may also save a copy of the work book as a soft copy.
8. Do not make your work book clumsy and overloaded. Information should be retrievable effortlessly.
9. It will be a good idea to take advice of a mentor and consultant in case of doubt.

10. If a page has become completely outdated, paste a plain paper over it and write again.

11. It is advisable to keep photocopies of all important documents. Collect visiting cards of your advisors/consultants like C.A.s, Advocates, Insurance Agent, and Brokers etc.

12. Keep clear copies of your PAN CARD, AADHAR CARD, Membership Cards, Passport etc. handy.

13. Obtain/ download latest bank statements, holding statements with mutual funds / demat accounts etc.

14. It is not mandatory to fill in all of them in this work book. Write whatever is relevant to you.

I hope you like this workbook.

You may connect with me at **lionpawankr@gmail.com**

PART – I

BASIC INFORMATION

Succession Planning Is A Process. It's Not A One Time Event

PART – I

BASIC INFORMATION

MY FAMILY MEMBERS

MY NAME IS:-	
AS PER PAN CARD	
AS PER AADHAR CARD	
AS PER PASSPORT	
Birth Date	
Blood Group	

NAME OF THE SPOUSE	
AS PER PAN CARD	
AS PER AADHAR CARD	
AS PER PASSPORT	
Birth Date	
Blood Group	

Name of the Children	Mobile No.	Birth Date	PAN No.	Aadhar No.
1.				
2.				
3.				
4.				

Name of the Grand Children	Mobile No.	Birth Date	PAN No.	Aadhar No.
1.				
2.				
3.				
4.				

Father's Name	
AS PER PAN CARD	
AS PER AADHAR CARD	
Birth Date	
Blood Group	

Mother's Name	
AS PER PAN CARD	
AS PER AADHAR CARD	

Birth Date	
Blood Group	

Mother's Maiden Name	

NAME OF THE BROTHERS	Mobile No.	Birth Date	PAN No.	Aadhar No.
1.				
2.				
3.				
4.				

NAME OF THE SISTERS	Mobile No.	Birth Date	PAN No.	Aadhar No.
1.				
2.				
3.				
4.				

EX-SPOUSE NAME	
AS PER PAN CARD	
AS PER AADHAR CARD	
AS PER PASSPORT	
Birth Date	
Blood Group	

CLOSE FRIENDS	Address	Mobile No.
1.		
2.		
3.		
4.		
5.		
6.		

NAME OF THE BUSINESS PARTNERS	Address	Mobile No.
1.		
2.		
3.		
4.		

5.		
6.		

NAME OF THE KEY STAFF	Address	Mobile No.	PAN No.	Aadhar No.
1.				
2.				
3.				
4.				
5.				
6.				

EX-EMPLOYER NAME	Mobile No.
1.	
2.	
3.	
4.	

5.	
6.	

MY PAN CARD

Paste here a clear copy of your
PAN CARD

PAN CARD is a legal identity for various purposes. It is necessary to cancel a PAN card after death of the PAN Card holder unless it is required for any other purpose like filing income tax returns of the deceased.

Similarly one may require PAN Card to clear outstanding tax demand or to receive refunds. If there are demat accounts in the name of the deceased, ensure that the holdings in his accounts are transferred to either the nominees or legal heirs. It is necessary to inform the authorities like I.T., GST, Insurance Companies, Mutual funds, professional bodies etc. about the death of a person. In short, PAN is required to be retained till all connected formalities are completed, for examples, closing of bank accounts, demat accounts etc.

MY AADHAR CARD

Paste here front side of your
Aadhar Card

Paste here back side of your
Aadhar Card

Aadhar Card serves as a proof of your identity, address and age in applying for Government job or availing Govt. subsidies or even for booking a room in a hotel. It is a universal number. It can be verified from Unique Identification Database (UID) maintained by Govt. Now the e-Aadhar facility allows us to have a soft copy of it at all times for easy verification. It's considered safe mobile banking as it involves two-factor authentication.

MY PASSPORT

Paste here inside page of cover
of the Passport

Paste here inside page of
last cover of Passport

Passport is a must to travel abroad. The Indian passport gives you visa-free access to a host of countries. When you travel abroad, it serves as proof of identity, age and proof of citizenship as a passport is universally accepted. Passport of a child minimizes the risk of losing them in child custody battles.

Always renew your passport before the expiry date. It is advisable to renew it at least six months before expiration.

MY DRIVING LICENSE

License No:	
Issue Date	
Validity period	
Issued By	

CREDIT CARDS

Credit Card (1)	
Card No.	
Valid Upto	
Issued By	
Sanctioned Limit	
Cash Withdrawal Limit	
CVV Number	
Outstanding as per latest statement	
EMI/Loan if any	
Helpline Number	

Credit Card (2)	
Card No.	
Valid Upto	
Issued By	
Sanctioned Limit	
Cash Withdrawal Limit	
CVV Number	
Outstanding as per latest statement	
EMI/Loan if any	
Helpline Number	

Credit Card (3)	
Card No.	
Valid Upto	
Issued By	
Sanctioned Limit	
Cash Withdrawal Limit	
CVV Number	
Outstanding as per latest statement	
EMI/Loan if any	
Helpline Number	

Credit Card (4)	
Card No.	
Valid Upto	
Issued By	
Sanctioned Limit	
Cash Withdrawal Limit	
CVV Number	
Outstanding as per latest statement	
EMI/Loan if any	
Helpline Number	

ATM/DEBIT CARDS

ATM/DEBIT CARD (1)	
Card No.	
Valid Upto	
Issued By	
Sanctioned Limit	
Cash Withdrawal Limit	
CVV Number	
Helpline Number	

ATM/DEBIT CARD (2)	
Card No.	
Valid Upto	
Issued By	
Sanctioned Limit	
Cash Withdrawal Limit	
CVV Number	
Helpline Number	

ATM/DEBIT CARD (3)	
Card No.	
Valid Upto	
Issued By	
Sanctioned Limit	
Cash Withdrawal Limit	
CVV Number	
Helpline Number	

ATM/DEBIT CARD (4)	
Card No.	
Valid Upto	
Issued By	
Sanctioned Limit	
Cash Withdrawal Limit	
CVV Number	
Helpline Number	

MEMBERSHIP CARDS

This may include membership cards of clubs, associations, Gym, Professional Bodies etc.

MEMBERSHIP CARD (1)	
Card No.	
Valid Upto	
Issued By	
Subscription /fees per annum	
Subscription fees paid upto	
Purpose of membership	
Other details like holding any office in the organisation	

MEMBERSHIP CARD (2)	
Card No.	
Valid Upto	
Issued By	
Subscription /fees per annum	
Subscription fees paid upto	
Purpose of membership	
Other details like holding any office in the organisation	

MEMBERSHIP CARD (3)	
Card No.	
Valid Upto	
Issued By	
Subscription /fees per annum	
Subscription fees paid upto	
Purpose of membership	
Other details like holding any office in the organisation	

MEMBERSHIP CARD (4)	
Card No.	
Valid Upto	
Issued By	
Subscription /fees per annum	
Subscription fees paid upto	
Purpose of membership	
Other details like holding any office in the organisation	

RATION CARD

Card No.	
Head of Family name	
Units Allotted	
Income of Family	
Date of Issue	
Place of issue	
Issued By	

VOTER'S CARD

Card No.	
Date of issue	
Name as per Voter Card	

MOBILE/ LANDLINE PHONE

MOBILE/ LANDLINE PHONE (1)	
Phone No.	
Customer ID	

Deposit	
Tariff Plan	
Prepaid/Post Paid/ Family Plan	
Mobile company	
service provider	

MOBILE/ LANDLINE PHONE (2)	
Phone No.	
Customer ID	
Deposit	
Tariff Plan	
Prepaid/Post Paid/ Family Plan	
Mobile company	
service provider	

MOBILE/ LANDLINE PHONE (3)	
Phone No.	
Customer ID	
Deposit	
Tariff Plan	
Prepaid/Post Paid/ Family Plan	
Mobile company	
service provider	

MOBILE/ LANDLINE PHONE (4)	
Phone No.	
Customer ID	
Deposit	
Tariff Plan	
Prepaid/Post Paid/ Family Plan	

Mobile company	
service provider	

SAFE DEPOSIT LOCKERS

SAFE DEPOSIT LOCKER (1)	
Locker No.	
Name of the Bank and branch with address	
Primary Name	
Joint Holder Name	
Nominee as registered	
Rent	
Renewal Due on	
Keys with whom/where	
Contents: (1)	
(2)	
(3)	
(4)	
(5)	
(6)	
(7)	
(8)	
(9)	
(10)	

SAFE DEPOSIT LOCKER (2)	
Locker No.	
Name of the Bank and branch with address	
Primary Name	

Joint Holder Name	
Nominee as registered	
Rent	
Renewal Due on	
Keys with whom/where	
Contents:(1)	
(2)	
(3)	
(4)	
(5)	
(6)	
(7)	
(8)	
(9)	
(10)	

SAFE DEPOSIT LOCKER (3)	
Locker No.	
Name of the Bank and branch with address	
Primary Name	
Joint Holder Name	
Nominee as registered	
Rent	
Renewal Due on	
Keys with whom/where	
Contents:(1)	
(2)	
(3)	
(4)	
(5)	

(6)	
(7)	
(8)	
(9)	
(10)	

DISCOUNT CARD

DISCOUNT CARD (1)	
Card No.	
Date of issue	
Issued By	
Valid upto	

DISCOUNT CARD (2)	
Card No.	
Date of issue	
Issued By	
Valid upto	

DISCOUNT CARD (3)	
Card No.	
Date of issue	
Issued By	
Valid upto	

DISCOUNT CARD (4)	
Card No.	
Date of issue	
Issued By	
Valid upto	

INSURANCE CARD

INSURANCE CARD (1)	
Policy No	
Issued By	
Policy holder	
Policy Period	
Premium Rs.	
Beneficiary Name	
Relationship with beneficiary	
TPA Name/Contact No.	
Name of the Agent/Consultant	
Helpline No.	

INSURANCE CARD (2)	
Policy No	
Issued By	
Policy holder	
Policy Period	
Premium Rs.	
Beneficiary Name	
Relationship with beneficiary	
TPA Name/Contact No.	
Name of the Agent/Consultant	
Helpline No.	

INSURANCE CARD (3)	
Policy No	
Issued By	
Policy holder	
Policy Period	

Premium Rs.	
Beneficiary Name	
Relationship with beneficiary	
TPA Name/Contact No.	
Name of the Agent/Consultant	
Helpline No.	

ELECTRICITY /GAS ETC.

ELECTRICITY (1)	
Supplier	
Meter No.	
Type of Supply	
Customer ID	
Deposit	
Billing Cycle	
Helpline No.	

GAS (PIPELINE)	
Supplier	
Meter No.	
Type of Supply	
Customer ID	
Deposit	
Billing Cycle	
Helpline No.	

GAS (Cylinders)	
Supplier	
Customer ID	
Deposit	
Helpline No.	

NOTES

<u>PART – II</u>

MY BANK ACCOUNTS

Share information with your loved ones.

They will need it in your absence

PART – II

MY BANK ACCOUNTS

BANK ACCOUNTS

BANK ACCOUNT (1)	
Name of the Bank and address of the Branch	
Account No	
Type of Account	
Account Holder	
Joint Holders Name	1.
	2.
Purpose of account like salary, Pension credit etc.	
Nominee(s)	1.
	2.
Specimen Signature	1.
	2.

BANK ACCOUNT (2)	
Name of the Bank and address of the Branch	
Account No	
Type of Account	

Account Holder	
Joint Holders Name	1.
	2.
Purpose of account like salary, Pension credit etc.	
Nominee(s)	1.
	2.
Specimen Signature	1.
	2.

BANK ACCOUNT (3)	
Name of the Bank and address of the Branch	
Account No	
Type of Account	
Account Holder	
Joint Holders Name	1.
	2.
Purpose of account like salary, Pension credit etc.	
Nominee(s)	1.
	2.
Specimen Signature	1.
	2.

PENSION ACCOUNT

Name of the Bank and address of the Branch	Type of Account	Account No.	Operated By	Remarks

NOTES

PART – III

MY SAVINGS, DEPOSITS AND INVESTMENTS

Save Money and Money Will Save You

PART – III

MY SAVINGS, DEPOSITS AND INVESTMENTS

FIXED DEPOSITS, RECURRING DEPOSIT AND BONDS

Name of Bank/ NBFC/ Corporate with Address	Type	Receipt No and Date	Amt. in Rs.	Due date	Whether any joint holder	Whether loan taken or given as collateral security
1.						
2.						
3.						
4.						
5.						
6.						
7.						
8.						
9.						
10.						

11.						
12.						
13.						
14.						
15.						
16.						
17.						
18.						
19.						

STOCKS

Name of the company	ISIN NO.	No. of shares	Demat A/c No.	Demat Co.	Operated By	Purchased on (date)	Cost
1.							
2.							
3.							
4.							

5.							
6.							
7.							
8.							
9.							
10.							
11.							
12.							
13.							
14.							
15.							

DEBENTURES/ BONDS

Name of the Co & its address	No. of Units	Demat A/c No	Demat Co.	Operated By	Face Value	Interest	Redeeming Date	Remark
1.								
2.								
3.								
4.								
5.								
6.								
7.								

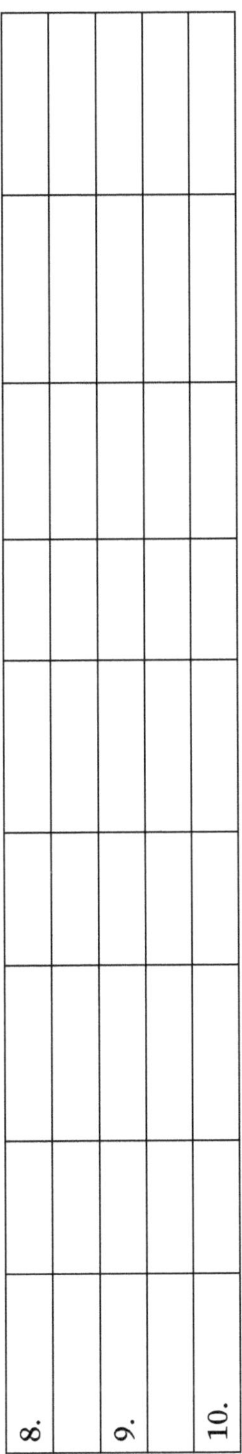

PUBLIC PROVIDENT FUND (PPF)

Name of the Bank/Post Office with Branch & Address	Account No.	Last updated Balance As on	Maturity Date	Nominees

MUTUAL FUND

Name of the Mutual Fund	No. of Units	Demat A/c No	Demat Co.	Operated By	Date of Purchase	Cost
1.						
2.						
3.						
4.						
5.						
6.						

7.						
8.						
9.						
10.						
11.						
12.						
13.						
14.						
15.						

CRYPTO-CURRENCY

Type	Exchange	Wallet	Custodian	Value

NOTES

PART – IV

PROFESSIONALS, SUPPLIERS AND SERVICE PROVIDERS

When we're in the midst of a fog and can't see the shoreline, we need a compass. Reach out to a trusted friend or advisor for perspective. We're not hardwired to go it alone. We need others to survive and thrive.

– Edward T. Creagan

M. D. MAYO CLINIC

PART – IV

PROFESSIONALS, SUPPLIERS AND SERVICE PROVIDERS

Chartered Accountant	
Name of the Chartered Accountant	
Mobile No.	
Email ID	
Firm Name	
Address of the Firm	
Landline No.	
Email Id	
Name of the Assistant	
Mobile No. of Assistant	
Appointed for which service	
Any original documents with him	
Outstanding fees, if any	

COMPANY SECRETARY	
Name of the Company Secretary	
Mobile No.	
Email ID	
Firm Name	
Address of the Firm	
Landline No.	
Email Id	
Name of the Assistant	
Mobile No. of Assistant	

Appointed for which service	
Any original documents with him	
Outstanding fees, if any	

TAX CONSULTANT	
Name of the Tax Consultant	
Mobile No.	
Email ID	
Firm Name	
Address of the Firm	
Landline No.	
Email Id	
Name of the Assistant	
Mobile No. of Assistant	
Appointed for which service	
Any original documents with him	
Outstanding fees, if any	

ADVOCATE/SOLICITOR	
Name of the Advocate/ Solicitor	
Mobile No.	
Email ID	
Firm Name	
Address of the Firm	
Landline No.	
Email Id	
Name of the Assistant	
Mobile No. of Assistant	

Appointed for which service	
Any original documents with him	
Outstanding fees, if any	

INSURANCE ADVISOR	
Name of the Insurance Advisor	
Mobile No.	
Email ID	
Name of the Assistant	
Mobile No. of Assistant	

INVESTMENT ADVISOR	
Name of the Investment Advisor	
Mobile No.	
Email ID	
Name of the Assistant	
Mobile No. of Assistant	

EXECUTOR OF WILL	
Name of the Executor (s)	
Mobile No.	
Email ID	
Name of the Assistant	
Mobile No. of Assistant	

FAMILY DOCTOR	
Name of the Doctor	
Mobile No.	
Email ID	

Name of the Assistant	
Mobile No. of Assistant	

OTHER DOCTOR (1)	
Name of the Doctor	
Mobile No.	
Email ID	
Name of the Assistant	
Mobile No. of Assistant	

OTHER DOCTOR (2)	
Name of the Doctor	
Mobile No.	
Email ID	
Name of the Assistant	
Mobile No. of Assistant	

OTHER DOCTOR (3)	
Name of the Doctor	
Mobile No.	
Email ID	
Name of the Assistant	
Mobile No. of Assistant	

TRAVEL AGENT	
Name of the Travel Agent	
Mobile No.	
Email ID	
Name of the Assistant	
Mobile No. of Assistant	

STOCK BROKER	
Name of the Stock Broker	
Mobile No.	
Email ID	
Name of the Assistant	
Mobile No. of Assistant	

CHEMIST SHOP OWNER	
Name of the Chemist Shop Owner	
Mobile No.	
Email ID	
Name of the Assistant	
Mobile No. of Assistant	

GROCERY MERCHANT	
Name of the Grocery Merchant	
Mobile No.	
Email ID	
Name of the Assistant	
Mobile No. of Assistant	

PLUMBER	
Name of the Plumber	
Mobile No.	

ELECTRICIAN	
Name of the Electrician	
Mobile No.	

OTHER VENDOR (1)	
Name of the Other Vendor	
Mobile No.	

OTHER VENDOR (2)	
Name of the Other Vendor	
Mobile No.	

SECURITY PERSONEL (1)	
Name & Address of the Security Guard	
Mobile No.	
PAN NO.	
Aadhar No.	

SECURITY PERSONEL (2)	
Name & Address of the Security Guard	
Mobile No.	
PAN NO.	
Aadhar No.	

SECURITY PERSONEL (3)	
Name & Address of the Security Guard	
Mobile No.	
PAN NO.	
Aadhar No.	

KEY STAFF	
Name of the key staff	
Mobile No.	

OTHERS (1)	
Name	
Mobile No.	
Nature of Association	

OTHERS (2)	
Name	
Mobile No.	
Nature of Association	

OTHERS (3)	
Name	
Mobile No.	
Nature of Association	

NOTES

PART – V

MY PRESENCE ON INTERNET AND SOCIAL MEDIA

You are responsible for everything you post and everything you post will be a reflection of you (Social Media)

– Germany Kent

PART – V

MY PRESENCE ON INTERNET AND SOCIAL MEDIA

Record your presence on social media like Facebook, LinkedIn, YouTube, Instagram, Google, Twitter, E-mail account etc. in the following format

Facebook	Username:
	Password:

LinkedIn	Username:
	Password:

YouTube	Username:
	Password:

Instagram	Username:
	Password:

Google	Username:
	Password:

Twitter	Username:
	Password:

E-mail account (1)	Username:
	Password:

E-mail account (2)	Username:
	Password:

E-mail account (3)	Username:
	Password:

NOTES

PART – VI

MY VEHICLES

I am emotional about engines,

if you hurt my car,

you hurt my heart

— Amit Kalantri

PART – VI

MY VEHICLES

MY VEHICLES (1)

Type	
Make	
Model	
Engine No	
Chasis No.	
Year of Manufacturing	
Broker, if any	
Purchased From	
Price Paid	
Whether Vehicle Loan taken	□ Yes □ No
Insured with	
Insurance value	
Expiry Date of Insurance	

Whether any Co-owner. If yes his name and address	
Details of vehicle loan and Insurance may be filled in at relevant section of this manual)	

MY VEHICLES (2)

Type	
Make	
Model	
Engine No	
Chasis No.	
Year of Manufacturing	
Broker, if any	
Purchased From	
Price Paid	
Whether Vehicle Loan taken	□ Yes □ No
Insured with	

Insurance value	
Expiry Date of Insurance	
Whether any Co-owner. If yes his name and address	
Details of vehicle loan and Insurance may be filled in at relevant section of this manual)	

MY VEHICLES (3)

Type	
Make	
Model	
Engine No	
Chasis No.	
Year of Manufacturing	
Broker, if any	
Purchased From	
Price Paid	

Whether Vehicle Loan taken	□ Yes □ No
Insured with	
Insurance value	
Expiry Date of Insurance	
Whether any Co-owner. If yes his name and address	
Details of vehicle loan and Insurance may be filled in at relevant section of this manual)	

The above information is kept for each vehicle. Vehicle includes cars, Scooter, Motor Cycle, Trucks, and Boat etc.

NOTES

PART – VII

TAXATION AND STATUTORY INFORMATION

The hardest thing in the world to understand is the
Income Tax

– Albert Einstein

PART – VII

TAXATION AND STATUTORY INFORMATION

My PAN No.	
My TAN No.	
My Profession Tax Registration No.	
My Company Provident Fund Registration No.	
My ESIC Registration No.	
My G.S.T. No. is	
Details of my GST Return	
My DIN No. is	

My Income Tax details:-

Assessment year	Returned filed on	Refund Claimed	Outstanding, if any	Whether rectification applied for	Whether appeal preferred

NOTES

PART – VIII

INSURANCE

You don't buy life insurance because you're going to die,

but because those you love

are going to live

PART – VIII

INSURANCE

LIFE INSURANCE (1)	
Policy No.	
Date of Issue	
Date of maturity	
Issued By	
Amount Insured	
Premium	
Nominee	
Relation	
Type of Policy and Salient Features	
Purchased through	
Whether Pledged	
Helpline No.	

LIFE INSURANCE (2)	
Policy No.	
Date of Issue	
Date of maturity	
Issued By	
Amount Insured	
Premium	
Nominee	
Relation	

Type of Policy and Salient Features	
Purchased through	
Whether Pledged	
Helpline No.	

LIFE INSURANCE (3)	
Policy No.	
Date of Issue	
Date of maturity	
Issued By	
Amount Insured	
Premium	
Nominee	
Relation	
Type of Policy and Salient Features	
Purchased through	
Whether Pledged	
Helpline No.	

HEALTH INSURANCE (1)	
Name of the Policy	
Policy No.	
Date of Issue	
Date of maturity	
Issued By	
Amount Covered	

Premium	
Nominee	
Relation	
Type of Policy and Salient Features	
Name of TPA	
Helpline No.	

HEALTH INSURANCE (2)	
Name of the Policy	
Policy No.	
Date of Issue	
Date of maturity	
Issued By	
Amount Covered	
Premium	
Nominee	
Relation	
Type of Policy and Salient Features	
Name of TPA	
Helpline No.	

HEALTH INSURANCE (3)	
Name of the Policy	
Policy No.	
Date of Issue	
Date of maturity	

Issued By	
Amount Covered	
Premium	
Nominee	
Relation	
Type of Policy and Salient Features	
Name of TPA	
Helpline No.	

VEHICLE INSURANCE (1)	
Vehicle Details	
Policy Issued By	
Policy No.	
Amount Insured	
Date of Issue	
Date of Expiry	
Premium	
Helpline No.	
Remarks	
Salient Features	

VEHICLE INSURANCE (2)	
Vehicle Details	
Policy Issued By	
Policy No.	
Amount Insured	

Date of Issue	
Date of Expiry	
Premium	
Helpline No.	
Remarks	
Salient Features	

VEHICLE INSURANCE (3)	
Vehicle Details	
Policy Issued By	
Policy No.	
Amount Insured	
Date of Issue	
Date of Expiry	
Premium	
Helpline No.	
Remarks	
Salient Features	

INDEMNITY POLICY	
Policy No.	
Issued By	
Amount Covered	
Date of Issue	
Date of Expiry	
Helpline No.	

Premium	
Salient Features	

OTHER INSURANCE POLICY (LIKE FIRE, THEFT ETC.)	
OTHER INSURANCE POLICY (1)	
Policy No.	
Issued By	
Amount Covered	
Date of Issue	
Date of Expiry	
Premium	
Helpline No.	
For which properties	1.
	2.
	3.
Salient Features	

OTHER INSURANCE POLICY (2)	
Policy No.	
Issued By	
Amount Covered	
Date of Issue	
Date of Expiry	
Premium	
Helpline No.	

For which properties	1.
	2.
	3.
Salient Features	

OTHER INSURANCE POLICY (3)	
Policy No.	
Issued By	
Amount Covered	
Date of Issue	
Date of Expiry	
Premium	
Helpline No.	
For which properties	1.
	2.
	3.
Salient Features	

NOTES

PART – IX

IMMOVABLE PROPERTIES

Private ownership of property is vital to both our freedom and our prosperity

Cathy McMorris Rodgers

PART – IX

IMMOVABLE PROPERTIES

IMMOVABLE PROPERTIES (1)	
Property Type	
Property Location	
Area	
Market Value of Property	
Whether Mortgaged (if yes full details like loan outstanding, rate of interest)	
Date of Acquisition	
Cost when acquired	
Agreement/ Certificate/ Property Card	
Property Tax paid /Due	
Insurance Policy issued by	
Date of Issue	
Date of Expiry	
Amount Covered	
Whether Property Registered?	
Whether rented or self-occupied	
Salient Features	

IMMOVABLE PROPERTIES (2)	
Property Type	
Property Location	
Area	
Market Value of Property	

Whether Mortgaged (if yes full details like loan outstanding, rate of interest)	
Date of Acquisition	
Cost when acquired	
Agreement/ Certificate/ Property Card	
Property Tax paid /Due	
Insurance Policy issued by	
Date of Issue	
Date of Expiry	
Amount Covered	
Whether Property Registered?	
Whether rented or self-occupied	
Salient Features	

IMMOVABLE PROPERTIES (3)	
Property Type	
Property Location	
Area	
Market Value of Property	
Whether Mortgaged (if yes full details like loan outstanding, rate of interest)	
Date of Acquisition	
Cost when acquired	
Agreement/ Certificate/ Property Card	
Property Tax paid /Due	
Insurance Policy issued by	
Date of Issue	
Date of Expiry	
Amount Covered	

Whether Property Registered?	
Whether rented or self-occupied	
Salient Features	

IMMOVABLE PROPERTIES (4)	
Property Type	
Property Location	
Area	
Market Value of Property	
Whether Mortgaged (if yes full details like loan outstanding, rate of interest)	
Date of Acquisition	
Cost when acquired	
Agreement/ Certificate/ Property Card	
Property Tax paid /Due	
Insurance Policy issued by	
Date of Issue	
Date of Expiry	
Amount Covered	
Whether Property Registered?	
Whether rented or self-occupied	
Salient Features	

NOTES

PART – X

MOVABLE PROPERTIES

Every right implies a responsibility; Every opportunity, an obligation, Every possession, a duty.

John D. Rockefeller

PART – X

MOVABLE PROPERTIES

PRECIOUS METALS (1)	
Type	
Weight	
Design	
Purchased On	
Cost	
Invoice No and Date of Invoice	
Approx. Market Value	
Location	
Any valuation report	

PRECIOUS METALS (2)	
Type	
Weight	
Design	
Purchased On	
Cost	
Invoice No and Date of Invoice	
Approx. Market Value	
Location	
Any valuation report	

PRECIOUS METALS (3)	
Type	
Weight	
Design	
Purchased On	
Cost	
Invoice No and Date of Invoice	
Approx. Market Value	
Location	
Any valuation report	

PRECIOUS METALS (4)	
Type	
Weight	
Design	
Purchased On	
Cost	
Invoice No and Date of Invoice	
Approx. Market Value	
Location	
Any valuation report	

DEBTORS AND RECEIVABLES (1)	
Name of Borrower	
Address of Borrower	
PAN of Borrower	
Date of Lending	
Evidenced By	
Secured By	
Terms of Lending	

Amount Given	
Purpose of Loan	
Details like confirmation, Bill of exchange or post-dated cheque	
Interest Received upto	1
	2
	3
	4
	5
	6

DEBTORS AND RECEIVABLE (2)	
Name of Borrower	
Address of Borrower	
PAN of Borrower	
Date of Lending	
Evidenced By	
Secured By	
Terms of Lending	
Amount Given	
Purpose of Loan	
Details like confirmation, Bill of exchange or post-dated cheque	
Interest Received upto	1
	2
	3
	4
	5
	6

DEBTORS AND RECEIVABLE (3)	
Name of Borrower	
Address of Borrower	
PAN of Borrower	
Date of Lending	
Evidenced By	
Secured By	
Terms of Lending	
Amount Given	
Purpose of Loan	
Details like confirmation, Bill of exchange or post-dated cheque	
Interest Received upto	1
	2
	3
	4
	5
	6

DEBTORS AND RECEIVABLE (4)	
Name of Borrower	
Address of Borrower	
PAN of Borrower	
Date of Lending	
Evidenced By	
Secured By	
Terms of Lending	
Amount Given	
Purpose of Loan	

Details like confirmation, Bill of exchange or post-dated cheque	
Interest Received upto	1
	2
	3
	4
	5
	6

DEBTORS AND RECEIVABLE (5)	
Name of Borrower	
Address of Borrower	
PAN of Borrower	
Date of Lending	
Evidenced By	
Secured By	
Terms of Lending	
Amount Given	
Purpose of Loan	
Details like confirmation, Bill of exchange or post-dated cheque	
Interest Received upto	1
	2
	3
	4
	5
	6

DEBTORS AND RECEIVABLE (6)	
Name of Borrower	
Address of Borrower	
PAN of Borrower	
Date of Lending	
Evidenced By	
Secured By	
Terms of Lending	
Amount Given	
Purpose of Loan	
Details like confirmation, Bill of exchange or post-dated cheque	
Interest Received upto	1
	2
	3
	4
	5
	6

NOTES

PART – XI

BORROWINGS, GUARANTEES AND OTHER LIABILITIES

Borrowing money is a temporary solution that often leads to a permanent problem.

PART – XI

BORROWINGS, GUARANTEES AND OTHER LIABILITIES

Secured Loans (1)	
Borrowed from	
Date of Borrowing	
Security	
Amount	
Rate of Interest	
Period of Loan	
Repayment Schedule (like EMIs)	
Purpose of loan	
Location of Security	

Secured Loans (2)	
Borrowed from	
Date of Borrowing	
Security	
Amount	
Rate of Interest	
Period of Loan	
Repayment Schedule (like EMIs)	
Purpose of loan	
Location of Security	

Secured Loans (3)	
Borrowed from	
Date of Borrowing	
Security	
Amount	
Rate of Interest	
Period of Loan	
Repayment Schedule (like EMIs)	
Purpose of loan	
Location of Security	

Secured Loans (4)	
Borrowed from	
Date of Borrowing	
Security	
Amount	
Rate of Interest	
Period of Loan	
Repayment Schedule (like EMIs)	
Purpose of loan	
Location of Security	

Unsecured Loans (1)	
Borrowed from	
PAN NO. of Lender	
Date of Borrowing	
Amount	
Rate of Interest	
Whether any P.D.C. given?	
Repayment Schedule	
Purpose of Loan	

Unsecured Loans (2)	
Borrowed from	
PAN NO. of Lender	
Date of Borrowing	
Amount	
Rate of Interest	
Whether any P.D.C. given?	
Repayment Schedule	
Purpose of Loan	

Unsecured Loans (3)	
Borrowed from	
PAN NO. of Lender	
Date of Borrowing	
Amount	
Rate of Interest	
Whether any P.D.C. given?	
Repayment Schedule	
Purpose of Loan	

Unsecured Loans (4)	
Borrowed from	
PAN NO. of Lender	
Date of Borrowing	
Amount	
Rate of Interest	
Whether any P.D.C. given?	
Repayment Schedule	
Purpose of Loan	

GUARANTEE GIVEN (1)	
On behalf Of	
To Whom	
Amount Guaranteed	
Date of Guarantee	
Purpose	
Details of Guarantee	
Any security obtained	

GUARANTEE GIVEN (2)	
On behalf Of	
To Whom	
Amount Guaranteed	
Date of Guarantee	
Purpose	
Details of Guarantee	
Any security obtained	

GUARANTEE GIVEN (3)	
On behalf Of	
To Whom	
Amount Guaranteed	
Date of Guarantee	
Purpose	
Details of Guarantee	
Any security obtained	

GUARANTEE GIVEN (4)	
On behalf Of	
To Whom	

Amount Guaranteed	
Date of Guarantee	
Purpose	
Details of Guarantee	
Any security obtained	

NOTES

PART – XII

WILL AND POWER OF ATTORNEY

"Record management is knowing what you have, where you have it and how long you have to keep it."

Anon

PART – XII

WILL AND POWER OF ATTORNEY

WILL	
Executed On	
Notarised By	
Registration details	
Prepared By	
Executer(s)	
Will Kept at	

CODICIL	
Executed On	
Notarised By	
Registration details	
Prepared By	
Executer(s)	
Will Kept at	

POWER OF ATTORNEY (1)	
Executed On	
Notarised By	
Registration details	
Prepared By	
Executer(s)	
POA Kept at	
Purpose of POA	

POWER OF ATTORNEY (2)	
Executed On	
Notarised By	
Registration details	
Prepared By	
Executer(s)	
POA Kept at	
Purpose of POA	

POWER OF ATTORNEY (3)	
Executed On	
Notarised By	
Registration details	
Prepared By	
Executer(s)	
POA Kept at	
Purpose of POA	

NOTES

PART – XIII

BUSINESS INFORMATION

If you are in business,

Know your legal duties

And responsibilities

PART – XIII

BUSINESS INFORMATION

I am /was partner in the following firm/LLP: –

FIRM/LLP (1)	
Name of the Firm	
Registration No.	
PAN No. of the firm	
TAN No. of the firm	
GST No. of the firm	
MSME Registration No.	
Shop & Establishment License No.	
P.F. Registration No.	
ESIC Registration No.	
Import Export Registration No.	
Business of the Firm	
Partnership Date Executed on	
Retired On	
Profit/ Loss Sharing Ratio	
Name of the Partners	1
	2
	3
Capital Invested	
Loan Given	
Interest on Loan	
Account Settled upto	

Latest Balance Sheet Kept at	
Other details	

FIRM/LLP (2)	
Name of the Firm	
Registration No.	
PAN No. of the firm	
TAN No. of the firm	
GST No. of the firm	
MSME Registration No.	
Shop & Establishment License No.	
P.F. Registration No.	
ESIC Registration No.	
Import Export Registration No.	
Business of the Firm	
Partnership Date Executed on	
Retired On	
Profit/ Loss Sharing Ratio	
Name of the Partners	1
	2
	3
Capital Invested	
Loan Given	
Interest on Loan	
Account Settled upto	
Latest Balance Sheet Kept at	
Other details	

FIRM/LLP (3)	
Name of the Firm	
Registration No.	
PAN No. of the firm	
TAN No. of the firm	
GST No. of the firm	
MSME Registration No.	
Shop & Establishment License No.	
P.F. Registration No.	
ESIC Registration No.	
Import Export Registration No.	
Business of the Firm	
Partnership Date Executed on	
Retired On	
Profit/ Loss Sharing Ratio	
Name of the Partners	1
	2
	3
Capital Invested	
Loan Given	
Interest on Loan	
Account Settled upto	
Latest Balance Sheet Kept at	
Other details	

I am a Director of the following companies

NAME OF THE COMPANY (1)	
Address of the Company	
CIN No	
PAN No. of the Company	
TAN No. of the Company	
GST No. of the Company	
MSME Registration No.	
Shop & Establishment License No.	
P.F. Registration No.	
ESIC Registration No.	
Import Export Registration No.	
Nature of Business	
Shareholdings	
Loans Given	
Rate of Interest	
Remuneration decided	
Balance Sheet /Profit & Loss Account kept at	
Type of directorship like Whole-time, Independent, Professional etc.	
Other details	

NAME OF THE COMPANY (2)	
Address of the Company	
CIN No	
PAN No. of the Company	
TAN No. of the Company	
GST No. of the Company	

MSME Registration No.	
Shop & Establishment License No.	
P.F. Registration No.	
ESIC Registration No.	
Import Export Registration No.	
Nature of Business	
Shareholdings	
Loans Given	
Rate of Interest	
Remuneration decided	
Balance Sheet /Profit & Loss Account kept at	
Type of directorship like Whole-time, Independent, Professional etc.	
Other details	

NAME OF THE COMPANY (3)	
Address of the Company	
CIN No	
PAN No. of the Company	
TAN No. of the Company	
GST No. of the Company	
MSME Registration No.	
Shop & Establishment License No.	
P.F. Registration No.	
ESIC Registration No.	
Import Export Registration No.	
Nature of Business	
Shareholdings	
Loans Given	

Rate of Interest	
Remuneration decided	
Balance Sheet /Profit & Loss Account kept at	
Type of directorship like Whole-time, Independent, Professional etc.	
Other details	

I am Trustee in the following Trust:-

NAME OF THE TRUST (1)	
Address of the Trust	
Registration No.	
PAN No. of the Trust	
TAN No. of the Trust	
GST No. of the Trust	
Date of becoming Trustee	
Amount Donated	
Balance Sheet /Income & Expenditure Account received upto	
Type of Trusteeship	

NAME OF THE TRUST (2)	
Address of the Trust	
Registration No.	
PAN No. of the Trust	
TAN No. of the Trust	
GST No. of the Trust	
Date of becoming Trustee	
Amount Donated	

Balance Sheet /Income & Expenditure Account received upto	
Type of Trusteeship	

NAME OF THE TRUST (3)	
Address of the Trust	
Registration No.	
PAN No. of the Trust	
TAN No. of the Trust	
GST No. of the Trust	
Date of becoming Trustee	
Amount Donated	
Balance Sheet /Income & Expenditure Account received upto	
Type of Trusteeship	

I am interested in the following organisations

Name and address	Position	Joined on	Subscription Amount / paid upto

I have subscribed to following Journals, Magazines etc.

Name and address	Publisher	Period	Subscription Amount	Expiry Date

I am author of following Books:-

Name of the Book	Name of Publisher with address	Terms and conditions

I am shareholder in following non-listed entities:-

Name and address of the company	No. of shares	Face Value of Shares	Date of Allotment	Amount in Rs.

OTHER COMMITMENTS:-

1.

2.

3.

4.

5.

6.

NOTES

PART – XIV

MY ABRIDGED BALANCE SHEET

An Abridged Balance Sheet

Will tell you at a glance

What are your Assets and Liabilities?

PART – XIV

MY ABRIDGED BALANCE SHEET

A Balance Sheet keeps you informed about your financial position i.e. your assets, liabilities and networth. It may be prepared every quarter ended or year ended. After the death of a person, the successor or executor has to manage the affairs of the deceased. An abridged balance sheet gives a fair idea about the financial position of the deceased. It is shorter than a normal balance sheet. All details are mentioned under major heads like properties, investments, liabilities etc. An abridged balance sheet will appear like this:-

LIABILITIES		ASSETS	
Particulars	Amount in Rs.	Particulars	Amount in Rs.
Corpus /Capital	100	Immovable Properties	75
Secured Loan	100	Investments	75
Unsecured Loan	100	Jewelleries	25
Payables	100	FD/RD/Bonds	50
		Receivable	50
		Inventories	25
		Cash Balance	25
		Bank Balance	75
Total	400	Total	400

My Abridged Balance Sheet as on

LIABILITIES		ASSETS	
Particulars	**Amount in Rs.**	**Particulars**	**Amount in Rs.**
Corpus /Capital		Immovable Properties	
Secured Loan		Investments	
Unsecured Loan		Jewelleries	
Payables		FD/RD/Bonds	
		Receivable	
		Inventories	
		Cash Balance	
		Bank Balance	
Total		**Total**	

My Abridged Balance Sheet as on

LIABILITIES		ASSETS	
Particulars	**Amount in Rs.**	**Particulars**	**Amount in Rs.**
Corpus /Capital		Immovable Properties	
Secured Loan		Investments	
Unsecured Loan		Jewelleries	
Payables		FD/RD/Bonds	
		Receivable	

		Inventories	
		Cash Balance	
		Bank Balance	
Total		**Total**	

My Abridged Balance Sheet as on

LIABILITIES		ASSETS	
Particulars	Amount in Rs.	Particulars	Amount in Rs.
Corpus /Capital		Immovable Properties	
Secured Loan		Investments	
Unsecured Loan		Jewelleries	
Payables		FD/RD/Bonds	
		Receivable	
		Inventories	
		Cash Balance	
		Bank Balance	
Total		**Total**	

NOTES

PART – XV

DOCUMENTS

Incorrect documentation is often

worse than no documentation

Bertrand Meyer

PART – XV

DOCUMENTS

Some records are of a temporary nature while there are many documents of permanent nature which are useful not only during one's life time but even after death. I always advise my clients to maintain a master file of all important documents. This will ensure that they are retrievable when required.

At the top of the document file keep an index of all the documents with serial and page numbers. If there are original documents in the master file, you may do pagination with a pencil. The master file should be a box file of durable quality. You may have more than one master file if necessary. Keep the master file in a safe place at your residence (not in your office). A photocopy or soft copy should also be maintained as back up.

Sr. No.	Name of the Document	Location	Remarks
1	BIRTH CERTIFICATE		
2	DEGREE CERTIFICATES		
3	DOMICILE CERTIFICATE		
4	MARRIAGE CERTIFICATE		
5	PAN CARD		
6	AADHAR CARD		
7	PASSPORT		
8	ELECTION CARD		
9	DRIVING LICENSE		
10	VEHICLE REGISTRATION DOCUMENTS		
11	CREDIT CARDS		
12	OTHER CARDS		

13	INSURANCE POLICIES		
14	PROPERTIES RELATED DOCUMENTS		
15	M.O.U.'s		
16	WILL AND CODICIL		
17	POWER OF ATTORNEY		
18	PARTNERSHIP DEEDS		
19	DISSOLUTION DEEDS		
20	DIVORCE PAPERS		
21	HUF PARTITION DEED		
22	FAMILY SETTLEMENT DEED		
23	GIFT DEED		
24	COURT/TRIBUNAL PAPERS		
25	LICENSES COPIES		
26	BANK PASSBOOKS		
27	BALANCE SHEET /PROFIT AND LOSS ACCOUNT		
28	DEMAT HOLDING STATEMENT		
29	PENDING LITIGATION (1)		
30	PENDING LITIGATION (2)		
31	PENDING LITIGATION (3)		
32	PENDING LITIGATION (4)		
33	KEYS OF BANK LOCKERS		
34	CERTIFICATE OF APPRECIATION		
35	TAXATION RECORDS		

NOTES

PART – XVI

ESTATE PLANNING

"We don't live forever...

Our legacy does."

– Greg Plitt

PART – XVI

ESTATE PLANNING

Estate planning guarantees that all of your physical, intangible, financial, and online assets are distributed to the person or persons you want after your death. Estate planning ensures that your assets do not wind up in legal battles for years. Legal actions unnecessarily burden your legal heirs, siblings, and family members. Effective estate planning should be your top priority in order to ensure the smooth succession and distribution of your estate. Two most common methods of transferring assets to the successors are by way of a will.

ALL ABOUT WILLS

An individual's Will is a legally binding document that specifies how his or her estate should be distributed upon death. A person can take steps to ensure that his preferences regarding his assets and property are carried out after his death by creating a will or a trust. When a person passes away intestate, it can cause a lot of complications. Some people carry out writings they have either prepared by themselves or had written for them by well-meaning friends, family members, or professionals.

The heart of the matter is that the legal heirs and successors often face difficulties if there is no valid will or if the will or a portion thereof is invalid. A person's property devolves in two ways after his death:

According to the applicable law of succession, When a person dies intestate i.e. he passes away without a will.

In accordance with a will, i.e., testamentary

THE LAW APPLICABLE TO WILLS:–

A well-developed and codified system of succession laws governs the disposition of a deceased person's property in India. The Indian Succession Act of 1925 expressly applies to the wills and codicils of Hindus, Sikhs, Buddhists, Parsis, Jains, and Christians but not to Mohammedans, who are primarily governed by Muslim Personal Law (Shariat) Application Act, 1937.

Exactly what is a will?

A Will is a legal statement that a person makes during his lifetime regarding the disposition of his property after his death. The Will does not take effect on its execution date. It begins with the date of the testator's demise. During the tenure of the Testator, the Will is an ambulatory document that is revocable at any time and has no legal consequence.

Wills possess two fundamental characteristics

It must be intended to take effect upon the demise of the testator, and it must be in writing. A gift to be implemented during the donor's lifetime is a "Deed of Settlement" and not a Will.

It must be revocable at any time by the testator, before his death. Although Wills are typically used to dispose of property, they can also be used to name executors, establish trusts, and name testamentary guardians for minor children.

WHO IS CAPABLE OF MAKING A WILL?

Under Section 59 of the Indian Succession Act:

Every adult of sound mind who is not a minor is permitted to dispose of his property via a Will.

Explanation 1. A married woman may dispose of any property she could dispose during her lifetime through her Will.

Explanation 2. Persons who are deaf, dumb, or blind are not incapacitated for creating a Will if they are able to understand what they are doing.

Explanation 3.—A person who is normally deranged may execute a Will during a period of sobriety.

Explanation 4.—No person may make a Will while in such a state of mind he lacks knowledge of what he is doing, whether due to intoxication, illness, or any other cause.

Illustrations:-

A is aware of what is occurring in his immediate vicinity and is able to respond to familiar questions, but he lacks an adequate comprehension of the nature of his property, the people who are related to him, or those in whose favour he should make his will. A cannot make a valid Will.

A executes a document purporting to be his Last Will and Testament, but he does not comprehend the nature of the document or the implications of its provisions. This document is not legitimate as a Will.

A creates a will despite being extremely frail and incapacitated, because he is able to exercise sound judgement regarding the best way to dispose of his property. This Will is legitimate.

The following people are ineligible to create a will:

A person whose mental state is such that he has no notion what he is doing as a result of alcohol, illness, or any other cause, including lunatics and the insane.

Those under 18 years of age, or minors. A minor does not attain maturity until the age of 21 if a guardian is appointed for him.

By their very nature, corporations are incapable of creating a will, though they may benefit from the will of an individual.

What purpose does a will serve?

In the absence of a Will, an individual's property will be distributed to his legal successors in accordance with the inheritance laws applicable to him. However, the majority of individuals prefer to dispose of their properties in accordance with their own desires. Thus, it becomes necessary to create a Will. In addition to this, there are the following distinct advantages to drafting a will:

When someone dies without a Will, there is often confusion among family members and relatives as to whether the deceased made a Will prior to his death. However, if a Will is present, the only query that must be answered is whether or not this is the last Will of the testator.

A Will is unquestionably a private document. It is primarily an expression of the relationship with family members, relatives, etc. A Will permits the devolution of property in a personalised manner, as opposed to allowing the impersonal inheritance rules to take effect.

By means of a Will, a parent can name a testamentary guardian for his minor offspring. A testamentary guardian is a guardian designated in a will or other testamentary document. This requires further explanation. After the demise of a parent, the law often recognises the remaining natural parent's right to act as guardian

Nonetheless, if there is no surviving parent, the law gives considerable weight to the parent's Will when determining the guardian. Before appointing the proposed guardian as testamentary guardian, this issue must be discussed in depth with the proposed guardian as it is of great significance to the children's future.

A Will addresses the specific demands and requirements of family members. For example, a father may have two sons. One is robust, while the other has been disabled by a chronic illness since childhood. Both of these offspring would be treated equally under the inheritance laws. With a Will, however, one can provide somewhat more for a disabled son, a bereaved daughter, or an ailing parent.

Without a Will, even the most undesirable son will inherit, who left the home for disobedience, deceit, violence, etc., and may return to claim his share of the father's estate. Similarly, a wife who has committed adultery may demand her inheritance according to inheritance laws.

In the absence of a Will, property would be distributed in accordance with inheritance laws. The Hindu Succession Act of 1956 codifies the laws of inheritance for Buddhists, Hindus, Jains, and Sikhs. The Indian Succession Act of 1925 will apply to Christians. The Parsis have a distinct inheritance law. Muslims also have their own legal system. This, however, has not been codified in law and is instead based on their religious texts. There are two main Muslim denominations: Shias and Sunnis. Both states have distinct inheritance regulations.

It is unfortunate that the majority of people do not have a will. Even a visionary like Dhirubhai Ambani probably did not make a will.

To ensure that the wealth created by you is transferred as per your desire, you must make a will.

HOW TO PREPARE A WILL?

There must be a written Will:

A Will must be in writing. Military personnel on active duty for an expedition or in a war zone are the only people who are exempted from a written Will. They can make a will verbally if they like. The term "Privileged Will" is used to describe this type of last will and testament.

Muslims can make an oral will

According to their personal law, Muslims are permitted to make oral wills.

No specific form of will:

No specific form of will is required by law. The language employed should be as straightforward as feasible and devoid of technical terms.

Will need not be on Stamp Paper:

It is incorrect to state that a will must be executed on stamp paper, as the Indian Stamp Act makes no such requirement. Therefore, a will can be written on any basic sheet of paper, which must be preferably be of a durable quality.

Typing is not required but desired:

A will does not require typing. It can be written by hand using a ballpoint pen or a fountain pen. A handwritten will is referred to as a holograph and is legally valid. In a handwritten will, however, the testator's illegible handwriting is destined to cause some confusion. Therefore, it is recommended that the will be typed precisely with margins on both sides of the pages.

6. Cautiousness

a) Prepare a list of your remaining assets and properties after deducting all obligations, liabilities, and expenses when drafting a will. This will help you gain a clear understanding of how you intend to distribute the estate.

b) The Will should be written in the language best understood by the testator in order to create the appearance that the contents were completely comprehended by the testator's desires and intentions.

c) If the testator is illiterate, the will must be carried out in a language that he or she can understand.

d) Unusual characters should be clarified and explained in the principal body of the will. In cases where a testator disinherits and excludes his wife and other family members from his will, or leaves his entire estate to charity, it is preferable that the reasons for the bequest to be stated explicitly in the will.

WHAT LEGAL REQUIREMENTS MUST A WILL COMPLY WITH?

In accordance with Section 63 of the Indian Succession Act of 1925, "every testator who is not a soldier engaged in an expedition or actual warfare, an airman similarly employed or engaged, or a mariner at sea, shall execute his will in accordance with the following rules:"

The Will must be signed or authenticated in the testator's presence or by another person at his direction

It is important that the testator's or his representative's signature be placed in a way that makes it obvious that this document is a will.

A valid will must have been witnessed by two individuals other than **one who makes a will.**

WHO MAY SERVE AS A WITNESS OR EXECUTOR?

In most cases, the testator will name an executor in his will or a codicil:

To manage the estate and see that the terms of the will are carried out

If the need for verification of the execution of the will arises later, careless witness selection could be deadly. It should be known that the attesting witness could eventually be called to testify in court to show that the Will was executed as intended.

WHAT IS A CODICIL AND HOW DO YOU CHANGE THE EXECUTOR'S NAME?

Any document relating to a Will that clarifies, amends, or supplements its bequests is considered to be a part of that Will. If the Testator just wants to update the names of the Executors by adding a few new names, a Codicil may be all that is required and does not require revisions to the Will's main text. A Codicil can be used when the Testator wants to make changes to specific bequests, such as adding or removing legatees, or when the names of beneficiaries or executors need to be changed because they have passed away. The Codicil needs to be put in writing. The testator's signature and the signatures of at least two witnesses are required.

WHAT ARE THE NECESSARY DOCUMENTS AND PROCEDURES FOR MAKING A WILL?

Wills can take any form the testator deems fit; there is no standard format. It must be duly signed and witnessed before it can take effect. The Will must have the testator's initials at the bottom of each page and next to any changes or additions. It is recommended that each page be fully signed.

No need to pay stamp duty while making a will or a codicil.

Making a Will on regular paper is fine.

Attestation:

A Will can be witnessed by two witnesses who must be present when the testator executes the Will. The testator and witnesses must sign together.

A witness, however, can be a legatee under Hindu Law. Parsi and Christian law prohibits witnesses from being executors or legatees.

If a Muslim's will is in writing, he is not obligated to have it attested.

Registration:

Registration of a will is optional under section 18 of the Registration Act. However, it is substantial legal evidence that the correct parties stood before the registering officers and the later attested after verifying their identities. The Registrar/Sub-registrar registers Wills for a little charge. The testator and witnesses must attend the registrar's office.

Registration allows the Registrar or Sub-registrar to provide a certified duplicate of the will if it is lost or destroyed. If the Will is contested, registration enhances credibility.

WHEN THE WILL MUST BE EXECUTED?

The executor of the will or a testator's heir may petition for probate after the testator's demise.

The court will inquire if any of the deceased's other heirs have objections to the will. Probate is granted automatically if no objections are filed with the court.

A probate is a court-certified copy of a will. A probate should be considered conclusive proof that a will is genuine.

In the event that any heirs raise objections, a citation must be served requesting their consent. This must be conspicuously displayed in the courtroom.

If there are no further objections, the probate will be granted and only then does the will take effect.

NOMINATION

WHAT EXACTLY IS NOMINATION?

The act of nominating is referred to as a nomination. To nominate implies to appoint someone to look after the person's property after his death. For example, LIC/GIC, BANKS, Mutual Funds, Co-operative Societies, and so on.

WHO CAN NOMINATE?

Nomination can be done only by a Investor or Policyholder who is a major and holds accounts, investment certificates, Insurance Policies,

Bonds, Demat Accounts, Fixed Deposits etc. and the nomination facility is only open to those acting individually or collectively.

WHEN THE NOMINATION CAN BE DONE?

Nomination is done at the time of investment or opening an account and after that by filing a relevant nomination form.

WHETHER OR NOT THE CHANGE OF NOMINATION IS ALLOWED AT ANY TIME, AND IF SO, HOW MANY TIMES IS IT ALLOWED?

Yes, the old nomination can be removed, and a new nomination can be submitted without the previous nominee being informed of the change.

TO WHOM THE NOMINATION FACILITIES ARE PROVIDED?

Nomination is available to Individuals who are Majors (Minors cannot nominate).

Hindu Undivided Family, Firm, Companies etc. can't nominate

Nominee can't nominate another nominee.

Those who are holding assets on representative capacity (like Trustees, Liquidators, Treasurers, Managers of a Bank etc.) cannot nominate.

WHO CAN BE APPOINTED AS NOMINEE?

A nominee could be an adult or a child depending on their age. In the event that a person under the age of majority is selected to serve as a nominee, a legal guardian must be selected to serve in that capacity until the minor reaches the age of majority.

WHAT ARE THE RIGHTS OF A NOMINEE?

The nominee gets the right to receive the invested amount, securities, insured amount etc. in the event of the death of the original investor, but he does not become the owner of the same. The ownership will depend upon the testamentary will or any other arrangement of succession made by the investor or policy holder. A nominee is a mere Trustee of the investor or the security holder.

It is best to have the same person serve as both the nominee and the beneficiary of the will so that any potential disagreements can be avoided in the future.

As far as financial assets are concerned nomination plays an important role in the following assets:-

- Bank Accounts
- Fixed Deposits
- Bank Lockers
- Demat Accounts

If the formality of a nomination has been complied with, the transmission is done in the following manner:-

A.	Death of a Single Holder	In favour of the Nominee
B.	Death of one of the Joint Holder	In favour of surviving joint holder
C.	Death of all the joint holders	In favour of the nominee

If there is no nomination, then transmission is in favour of the legal heirs. However, if one joint holder dies, then transmission is done in favour of the surviving Joint Holder.

The above rule applies to fixed deposits and lockers also. But in case of a locker, before handing over the articles to the nominee, the bank has to comply with certain formalities.

DEMAT ACCOUNTS

In Demat accounts not only you can specify upto three nominees but also specify the percentage of share of each nominee. The presumption of equal distribution among the nominees applies if no percentage has been set.

The Rules which apply in case of nomination in Banks also applies to Demat accounts. In demat accounts, it is permitted to opt out of making a nomination. However, it is always advisable to provide for names of nominees. In demat accounts the signature of witnesses of the nomination are not required if electronic signature is used to sign an online nomination form.

When a thumb print is used instead of a signature, however, a witness signature is still needed.

The situation with a joint Demat account changes slightly in the event of the death of one of the account holders. The depository participant will freeze the demat account and distribute any residual monies to the beneficiaries' demat accounts upon receipt of a notarized death certificate.

MUTUAL FUNDS

When it comes to Mutual Fund Schemes, demat account rules apply.

However, there are rules about what will happen if a nominee dies. If the nominee dies before the mutual fund investor, the nomination is cancelled immediately. If more than one person was nominated, and one of them died before the claim was paid out, that person's share would be split evenly among the other nominees.

In case of death of the investor the nominees have to comply with the followings:-

- KYC process
- Proof of Death
- Signature of the nominee duly attested
- Proof of guardianship in case the nominee is a minor.

It is advisable to keep a copy of the nomination form submitted to the Bank or Depository or mutual funds.

FREQUENTLY ASKED QUESTIONS

Q.1   What is a Will and what are the benefits of making one?

Ans: A WILL is a written document in which you provide for:-

    a.   the administration of your estate/assets when you die;

    b.   the distribution of your possessions in specific proportions to specific people whom you wish to have a share of your estate/assets;

    c.   appoint a person or persons of your choice to administer your estate and

    d.   appoint a guardian or guardians for your infant children (if any).

    e.   In other words it is a document where you direct, who is to receive your property upon your death. If you have any real property (land) or personal property (cars, jewelry, money etc.) which you want to give to a specific person then you must have a will.

Q.2   Should everybody – working or non-working person, man or woman make a will? and What if you die without making a Will?

Ans: "Where there's a Will, there's a way....Where there is no Will, there will probably be family bitterness/family disputes." If people die without a WILL, then the law will decide to whom the property of the deceased person should go to.

Thus, every person whether working or non working, man or women should make a will.

Q.3   When should people make a will? At what age on an average?

Ans: Every adult, no matter of what age, should have a Will.

Q.4   How do we make this will? Is there a process to making a will? What kind of paper is to be used? What language we must use in the Will? Do we need other people to witness the will?

Ans: This is no prescribed form for a Will; it only needs to be signed and attested.

- Can be in any language; no technical words need to be used
- Two witnesses must attest a Will; one preferably a doctor
- They should sign in the presence of each other and the person making the Will.
- In India, the registration of Wills is optional.
- The Will should provide for the appointment of executors, though not mandatory.
- No need to pay stamp duty for executing a Will.

Q.5   Where should we keep the will? Should somebody in the family/or friends know where they have kept this will?

Ans: Keep the original in a secure location where it can be easily retrieved after your death. Leave a copy with the lawyer who wrote it for you, as well as a copy with a family member, a CA, or an advocate.

Q.6   We see lots of problems in families when the head of a family passes away without leaving a will. Is that true? whether things would have been easier if there was a will?

Ans: If you die without leaving a valid legal Will, you are said to have died 'Intestate'. Who will inherit your estate and in what proportions is determined by the law.

The law also decides who will have responsibility for administering your Estate. Such decisions may create dispute and some misunderstanding among the family members.

Q.7 Should we keep the contents of a will a secret? Or, can it be shared with people?

Ans: It is advisable to keep the contents of a will secret. However, it is not mandatory to keep it secret; it depends upon a person to person and on a case to case basis.

Q.8 Once a husband has made a will, should the wife also make a will? Or Can a Husband and Wife make a Joint Will?

Ans: No it is not possible to have a joint Will. There must be separate wills. However "Mirror Wills" are quite common. A mirror Will is when a spouse or partner make almost identical wills, for example, leaving everything to each other respectively should one partner perish and if both perish together then directly to their Children. If they have no children then to a named beneficiary. This is where major differences often occur. For example, the husband could leave his possessions and estate to his siblings and the wife leaves her possessions and estate to her siblings!!!.

Q.9 Suppose a person makes a will leaving his/her assets and money not to family but to an outsider or perhaps to a charitable Trust – is this will valid?

Ans: Yes, basically a Will is a document that states or governs the will of the person, as to whom he/she wants his/her property to be handled after their death. So the person in whose name the assets are transferred can be any person, an outsider or even a Charitable Trust.

Q.10   Wills are often contested by people. Can you enumerate some of the most common grounds on which they are contested?

Ans: Yes, Wills are often contested by family members. Some common grounds on which wills are contested are as follows-

a.   That the person making the will was not of sound mind.
b.   The Testator lacked testamentary capacity to sign a will.
c.   The person was unduly influenced into signing a will/ or a will has been made under pressure.
d.   The will was procured by fraud.
e.   The Will is not signed before two witnesses.
f.   The names of family members are not mentioned in the will.

Q.11   Wills often result in bitterness and fragmentation in families – maybe somebody thinks he or she has not received what they wanted or less than the other person.

Ans: Yes, it might happen in various situations. In order to prevent such happening, it is advisable to consult a lawyer who will help you to draft the will appropriately and give the proper explanation as to why only certain assets are given to a particular member instead of others.

Q.12   Have there been cases in which a will has been deliberately tampered with? Or, when maybe mentally unsound people have been fooled into making wills?

Ans: There are very few cases where the will has been deliberately tampered with or when mentally unsound people have been fooled into making wills.

Q.13   Can a person change a will he has already made?

Ans: You have the right to change your mind at any time. However, when writing a new will, make it clear that it is the most recent and supersedes all previous wills. If you don't, it might compound the case, generate huge misunderstanding, force such matters to go to court, and take several years before a definitive judgement is reached.

You can also add to your will by making a "codicil," which is a document that has all the same rules as a will. The codicil must be written down, signed by you and two other people, and dated. Even if you sign and date the changes, you can't change a will that has already been signed and notarized. Such changes are only legal if they happen before the will is signed in front of witnesses and notarized. If big changes need to be made, you might want to make a new will.

Q.14 What should be a person's state of mind when he makes a will?

Ans: A person should make a Will in a sound mind and should have the will Registered with the Registrar of Sub Assurances in presence of two witnesses. The registrar might ask for identity proof, a Doctor's Certificate, Residential proof of the person who has made the Will, identity proof of witnesses etc.

Q.15 Should we take the help of a lawyer or a CA while making a will or can we make it on our own?

Ans: The procedure of making a Will is very simple. If assets are few than the help of lawyer is not necessary but in case if the assets are many and the family is big and if there is a possibility of disputes than it is advisable to take the help of a lawyer. As "Do-it-yourself" wills frequently lack all the basic components required by law and may be Courts have concluded that it is invalid (for example, no witness signatures). or no witnesses at all). Many times, when writing a will, you may use ambiguous language that leads to lengthy legal battles ("My House should go to Sunita." Which Sunita should get it if both mother and wife are named Sunita?) Anyone who stands to profit from the will's ambiguity can jump in to claim a share. And if the courts rule in his/her favour, you will not want that situation to occur after your death.

Q.16   Does marriage / entering into a civil partnership affect my Will?

Ans: Yes, if you marry or enter into a civil partnership, your Will is revoked. This is because there is an assumption that you would wish to provide for your new spouse or civil partner.

This rule has one exception, and that is when you have made your Will 'in anticipation of' marriage or entering a civil partnership. If you are in any doubt about this, consult your Solicitor for advice.

Q.17   Does divorce / dissolution of civil partnership affect my Will?

Ans: Yes, if you divorce or your civil partnership is dissolved, any Will you have made is revoked but only to the extent that your ex-spouse or ex-partner is referred to. For example, any appointment of your ex-spouse or ex-partner as an Executor or beneficiary is revoked. However, your Will may still be valid. However, it's better to take legal advice.

Q.18.   Whether the Property is inherited by the nominee under nomination?

Ans.   No, Appointment of the nominee is like appointing a trustee. Property will be inherited as per will/if there is no will then as per provisions of succession Act.

SPECIMEN OF AN ABRIDGED WILL

The following is the specimen of a will for reference purpose. You must take legal advice before finalizing your will.

I am........................, a male Indian resident aged.....years, currently residing at.....................................having PAN. NO............ Do hereby revoke all of my previous wills, codicils, or other Testamentary dispositions, and do hereby declare this to be my final will and Testament, which was drawn up in Mumbai on this....... day of...................., 2023.

1. I am possessed of sound mind and am in good physical health. I have created this will of my own free will, independent judgement, and while physically and mentally healthy; I have not been persuaded, cajoled, or otherwise coerced.

2. My family consists of the following members:

i) ____.

ii) ____.

iii) ____.

v) ____.

3. Throughout my lifetime, I have acquired properties, and I am in possession of Movable and Immovable Properties as well as choses-in-action. Keeping in mind the dissension within the family and the potential for inheritance-related disputes to arise upon my death, and in order to protect the assets from needless litigation among my relatives and others, I have drafted this will. I hereby devise and declare all of the property that I currently own or may acquire in the future in the manner described below.

4. I hereby appoint my wife namely .... the Executor of this my Last will of mine. In the event that my wife............... predeceases me, my son.............will serve as executor of this will.

5. I direct that the Executor pay for my funeral and other funeral-related expenses, as well as my just debts, taxes, and other liabilities,

out of the assets I own at the time of my demise. The remainder of my estate shall be left to my heirs.

6. I devise and bequeath all my Immovable and Movable Properties to my Wife .... and of which she will be the sole owner for the rest of her life, allowing her to do as she pleases.

7. If my wife......................... predeceases me, all of my moveable and immovable property will be bequeathed as follows:

(A)IMMOVABLE PROPERTIES

My entire estate will be left to my son, whose name is ....

(B) MOVABLE PROPERTIES

i)Rs .... is intended for my daughter namely ....

ii)Rs .... to be given to my granddaughter, i.e. my son's daughter.

iii)Rs .... is to be given to my grandson, i.e. my daughter's son.

And after the aforementioned sums are paid, whatever is left, including any assets I may acquire in the future, will be given to my son ....

IN WITNESS WHEREOF I the said .... have hereunto set my hand at .... this ....day of 2023

SIGNED AND DECLARED BY   )

The Testator above named as testator   )

for his last Will and   )

Testament in the presence of   )

us present at the same time   )

who at his request in his   )

presence and in the presence   )

of each other have hereunto   )

set and subscribed our respective   )

names as witnesses:)

1.

2.

GUIDELINES ON GENUINENESS OF A WILL

The Supreme Court [1] has recently laid down principles to determine the validity of a will. These principles/tests have been mentioned briefly below:-

1. In determining whether the will is executed by the testator or not, it is not necessary to prove the same with mathematical accuracy. What is required is to apply the test of satisfaction of the prudent mind.

Meena Pradhan Vs Kamla Pradhan 2023 (9) JT 275: 2023 (6) Supreme 633: 2023 AIR(SC) 4680: 2023 AIR(SCW) 4680: 2023 (9) SCC 734

2. A will need not have signature at the end of the writing. Signature of the testator at the beginning of the writing will suffice. Likewise, there is not requirement that each and every page must be signed or initiated. However, practically speaking it is advisable that each and every page of the will should be signed.

3. The will must adhere to every requirement outlined in Section 63 of the Succession Act. The testator's signature or mark, the attestation of two or more witnesses, and the witnesses' recognition of the signatures are all included in this.

4. One of the witnesses is required to give evidence that testator and the other witnesses have signed the will in the presence of the testator.

5. The attesting witness shall confirm to both the testator's signature and the witnesses' signatures on the will in the testator's presence.

6. The testimony of additional witnesses may not be required if one attesting witness is able to establish the execution.

7. The individual who is proposing the will (the propounder) is responsible for successfully dispelling any doubts that may exist regarding the will's implementation.

8. When there are questionable circumstances, the "test of judicial conscience" is used. The testator's awareness of the contents and effects of the will, their state of mind at the time of execution, and their capacity for free will are all taken into account.

9. The burden of proof rests with the accuser if claims of fraud, fabrication, or improper influence are made. Even so, the proponent is still required to offer a convincing justification to dispel suspicion.

10. Suspicious conditions must be true and legitimate, not just made up. Shaky signatures, mental infirmity, unequal property division, or the propounder's large advantage from the will might all be considered suspicious factors.

Financial freedom requires more than saving, starting early or frugality. It's your mindset which determines how much you will earn and save. You need not drastically reduce your life style and save every penny. What you need is to have a budget; you have to learn skills to strike it rich.

This book will guide you step by step to develop right mind set, follow growth habits and meticulously plan your financials. This book will immediately help in the exciting journey of financial freedom by hand holding till the end. You will learn strategies to make your golden years really golden. This book will equally help those who are in profession or business as also to those who are thinking of starting side hassles and develop multiple sources of income.

This is not a motivational book. This is a practical step by step manual to make you financially free.

CA PAWAN KR AGARWAL has been guiding his clients and others to lead a life free of financial worries since last three decades.

"Estate planning is an important and everlasting gift you can give your family. And setting up a smooth inheritance isn't as hard as you might think."

– Suze Orman

PART – XVII

MY FINAL DESIRE

"If you would not be forgotten as soon as you are dead, either write something worth reading or do something worth writing."

– Benjamin Franklin

PART – XVII

MY FINAL DESIRE

MY PLEDGES

EYE DONATION	
ORGAN DONATION	
SKIN DONATION	

OTHERS	

MY MESSAGES TO WHOM I LOVE

MY MESSAGES TO FRIENDS

MY MESSAGES TO MY COLLEAGUES

MY MESSAGES TO MY BUSINESS ASSOCIATES

MY MESSAGES TO THE WORLD

MY ASPITATION FROM MY KIDS

MY LAST PRAYERS

BY THE SAME AUTHOR

1. 12 MANTRAS OF EFFORTLESS LEADERSHIP

2. ULTIMATE FINANCIAL FREEDOM FRAMEWORK (UFFF)

CA with over three decades of expertise, PAWAN KR AGARWAL's passion is to empower people to achieve financial independence, take charge of their lives and become self inspired leaders in their own right. He is also a licensed NLP practitioner and actively associated with Lions International. He conducts a session titled, "Ultimate Financial Freedom Framework."